# How
# VOTERS CAN WIN
# the
# PRESIDENTIAL
# ELECTION

GREG DANIELS & JOHN COCKROFT

DC Squares
Daniels & Cockroft

# Copyright

# DISCLAIMER

## Dedication

To all the registered voters intending to vote in the 2016 U.S. presidential election weary of the crooked path the current political process has taken us.

# TABLE OF CONTENTS

# INTRODUCTION

## WHAT MAKES THIS LITTLE BOOK
## (so refreshingly dang) DIFFERENT!

### OUR AUDIENCE

Our target audience is registered voters over age 40. Those with some life experience and who feel the type of president in the White House should be there for reasons beyond outward appearance and personality. You believe selecting the president to be a high responsibility, and you don't want to have to choose a president merely to defeat a less appealing candidate. You want a president you can count on. You want the process of selecting a president to be streamlined, without agonizing months of negative ad campaigns, dodging questions, doubletalk and mudslinging.

If you are a younger voter interested in the above, welcome. We believe strongly in the importance of younger voters who look beyond the surface. Regardless of age, if you aren't registered to vote, or base your vote on trivial stuff such as a candidate's appearance or personality, put this book down, pop in your ear buds and go back to whatever it was you were doing.

### 2016

2016—another U.S. presidential election year. (Insert big sigh, big yawn, or both!) The closer to Election Day, the deeper the political doo-doo.

Time. For. Something. Different.

Who the players are isn't the primary focus of this book. In fact, this little book is bigger than the 2016 election. What you have in your hands is a proposal for a win-win-win solution that could transform U.S. presidential elections from now until the Internet is replaced by something better!

What exactly do we mean by "win-win-win"? Glad you asked, voter/reader!

Win-win-win. Voters win. Candidates win. Even the media wins.

How, dude, how?

Read on, bro!

## THE PROBLEM

We have the greatest democracy on earth, yet American voters are embarrassed by nonstop name-calling and bickering among presidential candidates. We wouldn't let our kids get away with attitudes like that. Why would we want to vote whiners and back stabbers into office?

The problem is the set up. The current system of allowing candidates' ability to headline and the media's playing up to them to determine the outcome, rather than the voters, is as full of holes as your average slice of Swiss cheese.

It's time to wean voters off "Jerry Springer Show" presidential debates which only divide and diffuse the outcome. It's time to help voters discover what candidates really stand for so we can all vote intelligently.

Currently, candidates aren't automatically fairly represented by a biased media. Voters deserve to know what candidates are really about instead of watching in dismay as they respond to cheap shots out of raw emotion.

Debates resemble little more than a desperate plea for ratings, as if candidates are actors vying for an Oscar.

Yet this is no movie. This is real life, and the election affects us whether we vote or not. Voters can't afford to let the country get suckered in by well-paid campaign jockeys.

And if all this posturing and cheap shot-ing is for ratings... (Look both ways, lower your voice and lean in so as not to be overheard) It ain't workin', dude.

There. I whisper typed it. The present system of presidential debates is broken. It's not accomplishing anything. Candidates are misrepresented and people are confused and irritated, not informed.

We need facts, not hype, to make this judgment call regarding our nation's future.

Just how, you ask, are voters to cut through the crapola of political posturing, pundits, and advertising spin?

You're about to find out! I'm getting goose bumps just thinking about it! Hurry, hurry, read on! Don't miss a word!

## THE SOLUTION

Aha, here it is: the solution! Drum roll please...

Hold presidential debates in a game show format.

Hang on—stay with me here, I see you shaking your head and rolling your eyes, thinking, *aren't things trivialized enough without making the election a comedy?*

Listen, a game show FORMAT is NOT a game show, no indeedy! A game show format would set the presidential debates in a timely, well-rounded atmosphere that voters would crave and learn from!

A game show style presidential debate would actually force clarity and specific answers without the clutter. And because it would be enjoyable, more people would be on board with the candidates, and therefore, on board with voting intelligently. We can bring back the fun and pride in our democratic system, and we can all win in the 2016 election and beyond!

A quick overview of how:

# WIN-WIN-WIN

- VOTERS WIN: Voters can see and hear what candidates truly want to say without negative bias so you can decide how to vote intelligently

- CANDIDATES WIN: A game show format for debates with established time tables for answers would allow more candidates to identify what they want to share without being waylaid

- MEDIA WINS: The media would get more ratings and money because the public with be enthralled with the watchable and enjoyable new debate format

# CHAPTER ONE

### IMAGINARY SCENARIO FOR FINAL ROUND OF
### DEBATES: TOP 2 CANDIDATES FROM EACH PARTY

MODERATOR ("MOD"): "One of these Presidential Candidates is sitting in the secret square! The candidate who picks it first could win the White House for the next four years!"

The MOD waits until the applause dies down before announcing the top two contenders for each political party.

As each is named, paid hecklers "boo" and "hiss", while supporters cheer as if their man (or woman) has scored the winning Super Bowl touchdown!

We're having here, but seriously, ground rules would of course be established, for example:

• all candidates would be required to attend 8 debates every third week between mid-January and mid-May.

• candidates would be expected to attend each debate

• penalties for skipping debates could include only being allowed to answer a defined number of questions in the next debate

• failure to attend the final debate might carry a penalty of not having a full display of important PSA infomercials

While the above scenario is purely imaginary, imagine if Presidential Debates were packaged into a snazzy game show format such as "The Hollywood Squares". We could call it "The D.C. Squares." It's a legitimate format to capture the attention of voters without dragging them into a quagmire.

Top candidates from each party simultaneously appear on a screen with nine blocks. Questions and answers would appear on the bottom of the screen, typed by stenographers backstage assigned to each square.

Candidates simultaneously respond to questions within a short time limit. Response times are based on the type of question. When the time is up, the question is no longer accessible to any candidate or stenographer, but the questions and responses are posted at the bottom of the screen for TV viewers only; and on a device in front of the live audience as well.

Questions are taken from each candidate's website and voting record (if possible!)

## HOW DID YOU VOTE???

An example of a question not currently being asked (but should be):

"How can voters access the voting record of any nationally-elected official?"

If they answer "go to the congressional website," hold them accountable on how to find it. The Congress.gov website could be posted live on the screen and the candidates would have to find their own voting records!

We figure they can't. We tried. And tried. And tried! (Read our fiasco trying to find voting records later in this book!)

## FIRST ROUND IN NEW DEBATE FORMAT

Imagine the first round, with candidates' used to blathering and sidestepping direct questions. "Well, it depends upon your definition of voting record; what bill numbers would you be referring to? I suppose—"

MOD: SORRY, YOU'RE OUT OF TIME! NEXT QUESTION!

The candidate has 15 seconds to answer this question; the clock starts now. TICK, TOCK, TICK, TOCK! Come on, think, think, think! BZZT! Too late, sucker! Political eloquence and doublespeak don't cut it in this real-world, no nonsense "game show" debate format!

Smart candidates would start posting their voting records on the issues they feel are important right on their websites, plain as day, or face the pressure and awkwardness of looking like a doofus!

The audience would benefit from watching candidates survive by being quick and to the point. Candidates, likewise, can sharpen their game and not get bogged down in nonsense that doesn't help. Lest you start pitying the poor candidates being put on the spot, think of this; if they only answer questions, they don't have time to hang themselves!

Less is more, right?

"Evokation" of other candidates' names for more air time...denied! (Currently, if one candidate mentions or "evokes" the name of another candidate during an answer to a question, the candidate whose name was "evoked" is allowed to respond to the question ad nauseam.)

## Ad•nau•se•am

*adverb*

referring to something that has been done or repeated so often that it has become annoying or tiresome, as in:

"The current presidential debate system allows candidates to ramble and dodge questions ad nauseam."

FRANKLY, MY DEAR...

## ...answer the question directly!

Other questions would have up to a 60 second response time, such as providing specific details dealing with the threat of ISIS...

MOD: "You have one minute, beginning now." (Some candidates would rather face terrorists than timers, eh?)

Then, for "kicks and grins", the multiple choice questions... Kinda like "Who wants to be a Millionaire" without paying for Regis to moderate. Heck, get him to moderate, if he can maintain neutrality. (Greg and John would personally want to see Kathy Lee, but that's another matter...)

Multiple choice questions may deal with how much foreign aid currently is provided to a country, and whether the candidate supports a lesser amount for that country. The answer would have to be one of the following: strongly agree, agree, disagree or strongly disagree.

MOD: "Candidates, you have fifteen seconds to produce your final answer, beginning now."

Can you picture Regis smirking with delight at his favorite new moderator role? I know, this is more fun than it's supposed to be, but that's the point!

Let's face it: we need some pizzazz in our political machine if we want to capture the hearts and minds of voters. The current method of weeding out presidential candidates is as cumbersome as using grandma's mimeograph to run copies of political propaganda for the entire state of Florida (where you'd be better off having a second grader count dimples and chads!)

In our new system, we would have no more liberal media attacking conservatives, and vice versa. Objective questions and simple, clear answers, would be typed out as the candidate speaks by a behind-the-scenes stenographer and a campaign staffer/ accuracy verifier.

The tension and excitement are high. The timer is running. Cameras sweep the candidates, the audience, and the backstage action. Viewers win, audience members win, media wins, and candidates are put in a position of being straightforward and leaving off the garbage that shrinks their respect by fellow party members and naysayers alike! Grab the popcorn and get educated. It's a quick, fast, fun way to celebrate the best election system in the universe!

To eliminate speculation of being "under pressure"... at the end of any debate, a website and media outlets would post answers to the questions as they were typed in real time.

TV viewers and audience members could highlight a particular box to hear the spoken words of a particular candidate or read candidates' replies.

Town hall meetings would give candidates time with voters without timers, but the televised debates would be under strict, fair, and fun guidelines!

With short, relevant answers, voters know where candidates' stand and can vote accordingly.

The idea, as we dwell on it, is already watering the drought that past election years have dealt us for decades. No more candidates looking for opportunities to exploit the competition by weaving tired rhetoric into headlines; no more media cracker jacks dropping hypothetical landmines for sensational sound bites and headlines. Bad candidate, naughty news boy, no biscuit for you!

Fear not, media members! In a game show format, cameras will roll behind the scenes in the stenographers' room; on the stage; and in the audience for a second by second "documentary meets reality show" feel. Can you feel the energy rise? Can you see the ratings soar?

God. Bless. America. Capitalism is still alive!

Again, candidates will learn that if they don't answer

clearly, concisely, sincerely; they miss the opportunity to provide an honest, direct answer to each question. Citizens would rather see "honest by gosh Andy Griffith" answers than "Attila the 'Hitler' Hun" bullying tactics.

Frankly, this new idea would cause Political Debates to revolutionize into media hits. The media would be the heroes rather than the villains. They wouldn't have to spin anything (leave that to the Maytag repairman on the spin cycle); all the real answers in real time would get real value to the voters and viewers, allowing the media to polish their production values live.

(Insert Dick Vitale voice over) What a show, baby! I can feel the rush! I can hear the roar of the crowd. Time Out, baby, we voters need a T.O.!

# CHAPTER TWO

REMEMBER... **This little book is bigger than the 2016 election!**

You have the ONLY book that, if followed, could:

- keep elections manageable time wise
- save big bucks on campaign donations and expenses
- restore the people's faith in the political process
- boost network ratings during elections

## TIME IS ON MY (OUR) SIDE

Let's all join hands and sing that old song popularized by the Rolling Stones at the top of our lungs, "Time is on my side..."

OK, let go of my hand, dude, I'm getting uncomfortable. Sheesh! And you ain't no Mick Jagger, stick to your day job!

What I'm getting at is that time is on my side, your side, our side, and the candidates' side if we advocate a time limit not only on the debate answering time, but on the total allowable time to seek the presidency.

Candidates should only be allowed to announce their intentions after January 1 of the election year. By summer, they've been through a series of game show format debates, the public is informed and not sick of them by the primary election in August. *Bada-bing bada-boom!*

## SAVE BIG BUCKS

Also on our list was to save big bucks on campaign donations and expenses. With a streamlined, entertaining format for debates, there would be little use for hateful invasions by media wolves to cripple their opponents. The idea is that when a candidate is "losing" a game show style debate, they use the other tantalizing game show style debates to recover, or not, as the case may be.

**We support dropping the campaign contribution system and making it impossible to "buy" a candidate.**

Let candidates seek office for noble reasons and don't try to derail them with money or unfair attacks.

Think of all the money special interest groups and corporations would save on campaigns, and hey, their candidate may actually win on ideas that improve the country altogether! Woo hoo! More money for big business!

(OK, a lot of you downtrodden didn't cheer with me there, but to each his own!)

## RESTORE FAITH IN THE SYSTEM

Any company exec, military leader, school teacher, or parent can tell you: morale among the ranks is essential for maximum results. Such is the case in our political system. If the public's faith in the election process wavers, you suffer voter apathy, disgruntlement, and polarization of parties. Competition is good, when it comes to finding the best candidates, but an apathetic, disgruntled population sees one candidate only as the "lesser of two evils" which can take away from the effectiveness of government.

A fresh, enticing format for presidential debates would win the hearts and minds of the voters and restore their badly shaken faith in a democratic system which works if allowed to operate.

# CHAPTER THREE

## GREG & JOHN GO UNDERCOVER

You lucky reader, you! Your clever (and handsome) authors are willing to do the grunt work for you. We're not just proposing a snazzy new system for bringing boring and confusing debates to an authentic sparkling sensation, no indeedy! We're going to do our best to improve your knowledge base WITHOUT a revolutionary change to our currently dismaying political system!

We rolled up our sleeves and set out an extra pot of coffee as we struck out on a heroic quest to provide voter's with the most accurate, comprehensive information. We warmed up our laptops and travelled the information superhighway all the way to each candidate's website to get the scoop from the horses (or donkey's, or elephant's) mouth about what they believe are the critical issues facing our nation.

What each candidate finds worth posting on their website is revealing about their values and exposes which type of voters they're reaching out to. With that in mind, we'll list the issues in this book, but we recommend you dig through their websites yourself for details.

Here are their sites:
www.DonaldTrump.com
www.HillaryClinton.com
www.TedCruz.org
www.BernieSanders.com

Okie dokie, here's the skinny; what we'll call the "Top 10" of each candidate, if you will. Understand there are not specifically 10 issues listed on their respective websites, but hey, "Top 10" is catchy and trendy, eh?
In no particular order, here we go: We'll start with the Hefty Hairdo, Donald Trump.

Trump's "Top 10":
- Healthcare Reform
- U.S.-China Trade Reform
- Veterans Administration Reforms
- Tax Reform
- Second Amendment Rights
- Immigration Reform

Next, let's go to Hillary Clinton:

To refer to this list of Hillary's most important as a "Top Ten" may seem, um, brief: Anyway, they're listed alphabetically on her site.

Here's the short version, alphabetically, as on her site:

Hillary's "Top 10"
- Alzheimer's Disease
- Campaign Finance Reform
- Campus Sexual Assault
- Climate Change and Energy
- College
- Criminal Justice Reform
- Disability Rights
- Early Childhood Education
- Economy
- Gun Violence Prevention
- Health Care
- Immigration Reform
- Infrastructure
- K-12 Education
- Labor
- LGBT Equality
- Manufacturing
- National Security
- Paid Leave
- Racial Justice
- Rural Communities
- Small Business
- Social Security & Medicare
- Substance Use Disorder & Addiction
- Veterans, Armed Forces, & Their Families
- Voting Rights
- Wall Street & Corporate America

- Women's Rights & Opportunity
- Workforce & Skills

John fell asleep during the reading of this list. Greg nudged him, but the drool was evident on his collar. (John has a rather short attention span). Let's all sit up, wipe the gunk from our eyes, and cruise on down to "Cruzville"...

Ted Cruz' "Top 10" (Hey, it really IS 10; wait, it's only 9!):
- Restore the Constitution
- Secure the Border
- Stand with Israel
- Life, Marriage and Family
- Rein in Washington
- Second Amendment Rights
- Defend our Nation
- Religious Liberty
- Jobs and Opportunity


Last but not least on our list, the grandfather of politics, Bernie.

Bernie Sander's "Top 10"
- Income and Wealth Inequality
- It's time to make college tuition free and debt free
- Getting big money out of politics and restoring democracy
- Creating decent paying jobs
- A living wage
- Combating climate change to save the planet
- A fair and humane immigration policy

- Racial justice
- Fighting for women's rights
- Working to create and AIDS and HIV-free generation
- Fighting for LGBT equality
- Empowering tribal nations
- Caring for our veterans
- Medicare for all
- Strengthen and expand Social Security
- Fighting to lower prescription drug prices
- Fighting for disability rights
- Senator Bernie Sanders' plan for Puerto Rico
- Supporting historically black colleges and universities
- Improving the rural economy
- Reforming Wall Street
- Real family values
- War and peace
- War should be the last option: Why I support the Iran deal
- Making the wealthy, Wall Street, and large corporations pay their fair share
- How Bernie pays for his proposals

OK, voter, now you have what the candidates find worthwhile. Check out the details and be informed!

You're welcome!

## VOTING RECORDS???

Now that your dedicated (and as we mentioned, handsome) research/writing guru team Greg and John were bringing you, the reader/voter, a list of what each candidate finds important, we thought it would be important for you, the reader/voter, to have access to each candidates' voting record (except Trump; his voting record is non-existent!)

We chugged another overpriced latte, ripped the peels off a few tangerines, and with a mixture of "tangelatte" on our fingers and lips, set to researching how to crack the code to the deep, dark underbelly of politics: the voting records of the candidates.

We pecked away at our keyboards. Our tongues protruded from clenched teeth as we huddled closer to screens, sweat popping out on our handsome foreheads. Time ticked away. The election drew nearer. And still, our crackerjack team couldn't crack any secret mystery codes. Finding the Holy Grail of Voting Records was proving too complicated even for our superior skills.

We looked at each other. It was time. Time to call the... *government* (GASP) for help!

*Dun, dun, dun, duuuuun!*

# CHAPTER FOUR

## U.S. SENATOR STAFFER OFFERS 'HELP'

We called our local U.S. Senator's office* (who must remain unnamed for protection of the guilty). A young lady staffer, let's call her "Kelly," answered the phone.

"We're trying to get the voting record for certain candidates online, is there any source for that?" John* (his real name, he's guilty already) asked Kelly politely.

"Are you near a computer?"

"Yes."

"I'll walk through it with you. Go to Congress.gov and click on MEMBERS, then from there you can find the Senator you're looking up."

Just like that? Wow, maybe the government flunkies are earning their keep after all!

Greg piped up. "What about finding the differences between Sanders and Clinton?"

"You can search the bill," the helpful and knowledgeable Staffer Kelly replied.

"What would we enter in the search line?" John queried.

"You'd have to know the bill number."

Let me play that back in slow motion to give Greg and John time to exchange knowing glances. (Read in deep, slow voice) "Yoo-uu-d haaaave to knoooooow the biiiiiill nuuuuuuumbeeeeeerrrrr..."

Um, I can see you in the back of the class, waiving your hand. "How would you know individual bill numbers?"

Excellent question. *Uh, ah, welp... ummm...*

John cleared his throat and gamely asked the staffer the $64,000 question: "What if we don't know the bill number?"

(How dare we just jump into seeking a voting record

without a PRECIOUS BILL NUMBER??!?)

"It would be a little bit of a—you'd have to sift through a lot of information," the helpful and knowledgeable Staffer Kelly stammered. "There are lots of bills and key words."

Undaunted, John typed in HILLARY CLINTON as an example. He and Greg stared helplessly at the screen. No bill number. No information. No voting record revelation. No, no, nope, nada, zip, zippo, the Big Goose Egg.

"What's the immigration policy between Clinton and Sanders, for example?" Greg offered, still hoping against hope to get something useful out of the government.

Our diligent Staffer Kelly was apparently scrolling through the same murky waters. We could hear her pecking away. "I can see where Senator Clinton sponsored some 2,600 bills..." her voice trailed off.

The simple answer was, we soon realized, there is no simple answer. Finding voting records for presidential candidates, or any other office holder, for that matter, are well, unreasonable, maybe even unconstitutional...

I had a flashback to the time I wanted to get tickets to

George Strait's farewell tour. I called a few weeks before his scheduled appearance. The woman on the other end of the phone said incredulously, "Um, George Strait tickets sold out in 15 minutes the day they went on sale."

# "The simple answer was... there is no simple answer."

"I would imagine that there are probably resources outside Congress.gov that put things in layman's terms," Staffer Kelly declared with all the confidence of a first grader explaining the birds and the bees.

"What if we entered a candidates' name and an issue, like immigration, how could we find how they voted?" John pressed.

"If you're on any one Congress members' page, you'll see a list by subject. Look through the policy subject and you can see more than 26 bills on Senator Clinton related to immigration."

Greg and John both inquired about the list of important topics listed on each candidate's website and how to find how that candidate voted on bills related to those issues.

You would have thought we were asking her to perform oral surgery blindfolded without going to dental school.

"I've never been in a position to look up voting records. All I know is my Senator..." she stammered, adding, "Senator Clinton isn't a senator anymore, so her voting record wouldn't be listed."

"Wouldn't they be archived?" Greg asked, incredulously.

"I'm sure they are... somewhere."

An awkward pause, as Staffer Kelly and we pondered that.

Greg sipped his latte. It was cold. John gnawed at a tangerine peel. The peel gave him inspiration. He had an idea. "Forget the presidential candidates for a moment. Just for an example," John asked Staffer Kelly, "is your senator's voting record available?"

"Oh, yes," Staffer Kelly declared.

"We need help finding it."

We could hear Staffer Kelly pounding her keyboard.

"Oh my goodness," Staffer Kelly finally exclaimed. We

weren't sure what that meant. Perhaps she had been browsing bargains online, or sending a staff memo about us to warn other Helpful Staffers about our invasive tactics.

Staffer Kelly's "friendly but getting impatient" voice returned to the line. "The senate portion of the website, Senate.gov, still requires you to know the bill number, but to compare candidates' voting records, use Congress.gov, which has the congressional record of every single bill voted on."

Time to stick out your bottom lip and wiggle your fingers against it while making unintelligible baby sounds.

As John was ready to terminate the call, Staffer Kelly bounced in with a final tidbit of information. "Here's one last website for finding the voting records."

She rattled off the site address like she lived there every moment of every day. We asked her to repeat it.

"Senate dot gov slash legislative slash legislative..."

Greg was taking hand written notes; John was pounding away on his keyboard; our personal staffer had her Dictaphone; her assistant was using shorthand.

"Say that one more time?" Greg asked, confused and temporarily overwhelmed.

We recited the website address in unison with Staffer Kelly, like Vince Vaughn and Owen Wilson, just a couple of seasoned, middle-aged real-world white guys trying our best to follow along in the terrifying new terrain of political technology.

"Senate dot gov slash legislative slash legislative..."

Greg: Legislative Slash Legislative?

"Underscore home dot HTM."

John: HTM?

Greg: Underscore HTM?

Staffer Kelly: Yes!

John: HTM... as in 'Holocaust Theodore Marsupial?'

Greg and John exchanged glances. Had Staffer Kelly hung up? Was she rolling her eyes on the other end of the phone? Were we on speaker phone as other staffer's stifled guffaws?

John re-read his script for final verification: "OK, so that's Senate dot gov slash legislative slash legislative underscore home dot htm."

BINGO! You got it, old-timer! Congratu-stinkin-lations!

Here is the site for you, the reader, to click:

Senate.gov/legislative/legislative home.htm

Now that we had finally landed upon this desolate planet of a website, buried beneath 20,000 leagues of political ocean, Greg and John exchanged dutiful glances, wiped the tangelatte off their fingers and lips, and dove into the site with trembling fingers, beating hearts, and the promise of a rare and valuable discovery...

Oh, no. No. NO, NO, NO!!!

Sorry. Let me let you, the reader, in on what's going on as we explore the Holy Grail of all political websites listed above. It's, well... if you're not John Nash (a Nobel laureate featured in the movie "A Beautiful Mind") you may have as much difficulty finding bill numbers or something useful on this "prestigious quagmire from governmental hell" website as we did.

I wish this story had a better ending. Greg and John definitely wanted this portion of our book to be one of victory, of gaining the edge for the reader/voter; but alas!

We simply didn't possess the numbers of every House and Senate bill ever voted upon. Shucks! Epic Fail, us! We may not have what it takes to survive the political arena; thank goodness we're not candidates!

"These guys are hiding in plain sight," Greg quipped. John

slapped that quote into these precious pages, risking "evoking" Greg's name... in vain?

"They're playing 'catch me if you can' with their voting records," Greg, ever the Quipster, continued as John pecked away furiously, capturing the moment before he lost its significance. If we couldn't find answers, at least we were waxing eloquent about it.

## PAIN RELIEF

Lo and behold, while randomly scanning Google for help in finding voter records, Greg and John stumbled upon these two gems:

http://www.VoteSmart.org
http://www.OnTheIssues.org

Go there and enter a candidates' name. There are different categories to figure how they voted or how they stand on issues facing the 2016 election. Wonder why Staffer Kelly and others paid to find out this stuff aren't in the know?

No worry. Your helpful, friendly, and (yes, handsome!) authors are here to rescue you, the reader/voter, once again!

# VOTESMART.ORG

# ONTHEISSUES.ORG

## (plop, plop, fizz, fizz, oh, what a relief it is!)

# CHAPTER FIVE

*"These guys (elected officials) are hiding in plain sight."*
*—Greg Daniels*

### FUN WITH DICK AND JANE

Are you old enough to remember reading "Dick and Jane" books in school? Greg and John sure are!

Imagine the simple easy reader format of Dick and Jane books as it applies to the 2016 Presidential Election:

See Bernie gripe.
"Gripe, Bernie, gripe!"

See Donald dodge.
"Dodge, Donald, dodge!"

See Ted blame.
"Blame, Ted, blame!"

Hear Hillary deny.
"Deny, Hillary, deny!"

## Almost brings a twinge of nostalgia, eh?

## CALLING SENATOR SANDERS!

Having done so well trying to dig up the voting record of our local U.S. Senator, we decided to go for a real, live U.S. Presidential Candidate—Bernie Sanders.

We called the good Senator at 802-862-1505 in Burlington, VT. John keyed in the number on his cell phone and hit the speaker button. A young female recorded voice came on:

*"Thanks for calling the Bernie 2016 campaign headquarters, if you're calling with questions about the website, events, making a donation, or any other campaign related issue, please e-mail us, at help@BernieSanders.com for the fastest response and the most accurate information. If you have a suggestion or information to share, please put it in writing and send it to info@BernieSanders.com. Press inquiries? E-mail press@BernieSanders.com. To get involved in a political revolution where you live, check out... (She listed another e-mail addy) If you would like to make a donation on the phone, please stay on the line and the next available agent will be with you..."*

We were on hold. No hold music. Hmmm. Should we hum to ourselves?

We waited for the Senior Senator from Vermont to reply. Waiting. Waiting to contribute to his campaign, presumably.

Minutes ticked by. Tick. Tick. Tick. Tock. Tock. Tock.

Three minutes and twenty-four seconds. Greg and John joked and laughed as they waited.

*"The maximum recording time has been reached,"* the voice declared four minutes into it and the call was terminated from the other end.

Greg and John realized later that the call was set up to record the caller, rather than place the caller on hold.

We had been joking around about Bernie Sanders' Puerto Rican plan, the movie "Weekend at Bernie's" where a dead man named Bernie is propped up by his friends, and more... all recorded for the listening pleasure of some "Bernie for Prez" staffer to hear and languish over. Oops...

## THE DONALD

After that four minute waste of time, we immediately researched how to call Donald Trump. A Yahoo search revealed an entire page of ads. No number.

We went to Google and entered "phone number for Trump campaign headquarters" and DonaldJTrump.com came up with a form to fill out your name and e-mail in order to get the privilege of hearing back from the wealthy NYC big hair businessman turned presidential hopeful.

No phone number was listed anywhere we could find. Greg reluctantly filled out the form on the website, which displayed an image of the Trump Tower in lower Manhattan. "Are we on the Trump Trail?" John asked, laughing.

We came up with how many words rhyme with Trump. There are many, many. Most of which are quite funny.

Greg kept trying to fill out the form, but when it came to what state you're from, the first state alphabetically was ALABAMA. The menu wouldn't allow for him to scroll down to the other states. After about a hundred thirty thousand tries, Greg shrugged, sighed, and submitted the form as if he was an Alabama resident. "Roll tide, roll!"

Next, after Greg from "Alabama" finished his address, there was a COMMENT box. "Please call me" Greg typed and hit SUBMIT.

Trump's automated reply came back with a "Thank You for Contacting Us" generic message. We could feel the love.

## CRUZ'S TURN

What else is there for a couple pro's like your authors? On to Texas; that's right, Ted Cruz, pard'ner!

We squinted at another series of screens. TedCruz.org was summoned. Specific donation amounts were listed on the site. One that struck John funny was $25 $50 $500 $1000 $2700... Whoa, there, Texan! $2700? What's up with that? Not $2600, not $2800?

Is this some form of random intelligence test numbers designed to rank your IQ? Remember those tests where they give you a series of five numbers in no particular order, such as 25, 50, 500, 1000, 2700, what number comes next??? Again, where's John Nash? Maybe he can help! Oh wait, he died in 2015 (yep, we Googled it)!

It was time for a true Ted Cruz story. John leaned in and asked Greg, "you wanna hear a true Ted Cruz story?"

"I do," Greg dutifully took the bait.

"I was at the Ted Cruz rally a little over a week ago at Evangel University in Springfield, Missouri," John began. "I was too late to get inside. The building was at capacity and about a dozen people stood outside the locked doors, looking in through the windows, hoping someone would violate fire code and let them in; or that suddenly a small group would flee the building and allow them to come in. At any rate, here were a dozen adults standing outside a locked building like the runt puppies left in the FREE PUPPIES box after the good puppies are taken.

A woman approached with a Subway sandwiches bag and security let her in, with the comment to those of us runt puppies standing outside, "she has 'treats' for Ted Cruz".

Wow. So, all John needed to do was wear a wig, a skirt, and carry a Subway bag? WWJND? (What Would John Nash Do?)

Other than stories and jokes, no Ted Cruz number existed for John and Greg that day. A second donation page came up on Ted Cruz' site, this one begging for donations as low as $5. "Now he's reaching out to the common man," John declared. "I'd send him five bucks if he'd send me his personal phone number!"

# CHAPTER SIX

## BIG, BAD GOVERNMENT WOLF UNCOVERED

Here's the groovy part of this radical new book thingy you have in your pretty lil' hands: While it's a fun fantasy to run an election process like a game show, get ready for some TRUTH brought to you by our fabulous research team of one!

In all seriousness, most voters (and non-voters) feel disillusioned with the Big, Bad Government Wolf and its evil "Wolfling", the Election Process. This makes the election cycle feel like more like we're Little Red Riding Hood, trying to uncover this Big, Bad Wolf and its ugly child from underneath Grandma's bed covers.

To bust this hideous image, we propose that our idea of a "D.C. Squares" game replace current debates. D.C. Square's simultaneous answering approach would be fun, fair, open, and honest; with a level playing field so no candidate would be able to sabotage their opponents' previous comments.

## SHORTER ELECTION CYCLES=CLEANER RESULTS

If we put clothes in a longer spin cycle, does that mean they'll have less wrinkles? I dunno, I ain't no Alice from The Brady Bunch, but I'm convinced that elections can get fewer wrinkles with shorter cycles.

## THE OTHER GUYS

What we did discover is that in other democracies, even those recently able to have free and open elections, much shorter election cycles focus on the mission of a strategic plan of democratic (voting) action to whip their country into shape.

The result? Laser focus on issues and candidates. No dreadful marathons of political posturing and paying media outlets for air time and print space.

Some countries have streamlined nominations, cut the fat off the electoral process time, and determined how many candidates are allowed on the short list for consideration while helping constituents and candidates better understand and manage the issues.

The United States isn't the only country that believes in a strong economy, strong military, great education system, and other basic democracy-oriented community values and protection of beliefs.

Even the Middle East has more free elections than ever thought possible.

Tragically, in many countries, utopian desires have given way to ethnic cleansing, the Holocaust, political correctness, and other issues, causing many to feel that their lives don't matter.

There ain't no perfect system, y'all. Gimme free and open elections where candidates are treated proper-like and the integrity of all candidates are intact and based on the issues. Each candidate's voting record should reflect how they feel about the issues and the citizens that voted them in.

Then there's the deal with two main parties divided by conservative and liberal press in amazingly equal numbers. Because of nearly a 50/50 split, this perpetuates gridlock, which is especially evident in the fourth year of a second term president. This is historically the same regardless of which party occupies the White House during the dreadful fourth year of the second term.

*"The United States isn't the only country that believes in a strong economy, strong military, great education system, and other basic democracy-oriented community values and protection of beliefs."*
*—Greg Daniels*

# CHAPTER SEVEN

### THIS LITTLE VOTER

This little voter went to market. This little voter registered but stayed home. This little voter went "Wee-Wee-Wee regret ever voting for that joker in the first place!"

### "IT'S THE ECONOMY, STUPID!"

Even if it's not your first rodeo, any political cowboy worth their boots hangs their hat on the Standard and Poor's 500 Index.

Hang on to your hats, because historically in presidential election years there will be a 3% drop in the market if the incumbent is not seeking re-election.

The average return for the ol' S & P since way back in 1928 is 7.5% and goes all the way up to a whopping 12% when a sitting president is up for re-election.

But since 9/11, the numbers have sagged like the swayback of a Shetland Pony under Hoss from Bonanza.

The final year of a two term presidency is infamous for pardons, business as usual, and overall becomes a lackadaisical last round up. The economy, jobs, military contracts, foreign relations etc. are a smoldering campfire and the weeds are growing all over the Ponderosa.

In 1980, during Carter's miserably failed re-election campaign, the screw up was largely due to three factors:

- the economy
- high unemployment
- high budget deficit

Bush 41, George Herbert Walker Bush, lost his second term with his slogan "Read My Lips—No new taxes" but washed out under the tsunami of Clinton's counter slogan, "It's the economy, stupid."

Score one for Clinton's salesmanship. The end result cut Bush 41 out of a second term, and paved the way for Clinton's two terms.

Clinton put on the good face for the economy at the cost of cutting the military and tweaking the budget to suit his case.

Another interesting piece to this whole puzzle—party stereotypes are no longer in stereo. They're sounding pretty mono these days. They're simply not as true as back when your dad or grandpa was a young voter. For instance, the stereotype that Republicans are the party of business owners; Democrats are the party favored by labor; those are not as true as 50 to 75 years ago.

Hard-core supporters on both sides of the issue almost need to be removed from any sensible discussion. Sometimes it seems that no matter what you say, these zealots want it both ways, whether liberal or conservative.

Take away the zealots and you still have 90% of

Democrats and Republicans being reasonably... *reasonable.*

I can hear the historians crying "What about FDR?"
OK, OK, his results look much better because the nation was in the Great Depression up until he was elected and there was nowhere to go but up.

Bush 43 (George W. Bush), continued the mojo with the economy, but then the bubble popped. The jig was up. The Dow dropped. And down came the economy, cradle and all. Epic Fail for market investors.

Ronald Reagan, Dwight Eisenhower, and Bill Clinton all had economically "good times" throughout their terms. Again, if you get rid of those pesky 10% die hards, there can be much more dynamic tension needed for positive mojo.

Unfortunately, nowadays, each party wants to keep the rage against the other party hyped up in order to guilt voters into keeping incumbents in office to keep the other side from messing up the economy, military, education, healthcare, infrastructure, or whatever the political "flavor of the month" topic.

The existing "debate circus" format is a repellant to truly important new issues. Admit it, you 10% hard-cores on both party lines: both parties have failed U.S. citizens miserably.

To put it simply, we all need to learn to play together in the proverbial sandbox. No one party has all the good ideas. No one party has all the bad ideas.

### IS THE STOCK MARKET DEMOCRAT OR REPUBLICAN?

The stock market is impacted by elections. Elections are impacted by the stock market.

Though markets have averaged 7.5% annual increases for nine decades, some of the most interesting economic paradigms seem to be orchestrated by a handful of people behind the scenes. (Pay CLOSE ATTENTION to that man behind the curtain, no matter what the Great and Powerful Oz says!)

But instead of a big, scary face with smoke effects, these Modern Day Wizards of Oz use sophisticated software to invest, make a profit, and pull their money out fast enough to make Gordon Gekko jealous!

Campaign election committees seem to stoop to any level to get their candidate elected. Negative ads, attack ads, and lapses in honesty. It's a dirty business running a campaign.

Snippets from certain candidates are manipulated to sound as if the sponsoring candidate wants potential voters to perceive the rival candidate a certain way.

Confusion in different media including Twitter, Facebook, LinkedIn and website posts and blogs is rampant. Another common tactic is to circulate literature that appears to be official voter registration materials when in fact they are purposely made to trick even informed voters. I have long

43

believed that there's a rather simple solution to eliminate facts and super PACs etc.

John attended a men's breakfast recently. An older man was upset. "I got a PAST DUE notice," he said. "I panicked. I opened it up, and it was just a political party asking for money. What a crock!" Another man next to him shared a similar experience of receiving a fraudulent letter begging for political donations.

The government should provide Public Service Announcements on voting records during a candidates' time in office. For candidates with no previous public office held, list the issues posted on their websites and how they say they intend to vote on those issues.

Here's a novel idea: Each office holders' website includes an easily accessed "how I voted" button. For example, same sex marriage, abortion, immigration, gun control, etc. Did they vote for, against, or abstain? Each website should have a clearly identified voting record. No more "hiding in plain sight" as Greg likes to say.

In researching this book, we learned about 50% of respondents to Republican and Democratic websites believe their candidate will listen and make a difference. Both major parties have a lot of dissension in the ranks but the Democrats show less internal bleeding.

Democrats are better politicians. Think about it. They spin issues like a good Maytag dryer.

## JUST A SWINGIN'

More than a few voters identify with the John Anderson hit, "Swingin'" that is, they swing to either side of the political landscape. Some on principle; others perhaps just to shake things up.

Another factor determining the swing vote: 2016 voter turnout continues to trend higher than any election in recent memory. People want their beliefs, moral values and thoughts to be measured at the ballot box. Donald Trump is resonating with voters, whether you believe in him as a viable candidate or not, he is an alternative to the Republicans losing most any politically disputed ground.

Voting preferences are greatly influenced by various sources. Some follow talking heads on conservative or liberal news outlets. Others follow the lead at work, their circle of friends, or align themselves with family when deciding whom they will vote for.

It is more difficult to break ranks with friends and family, but is a fairly common phenomenon. For those not following strict party line voting strategies, an outsider may resonate because he is not an insider within the Beltway, where insiders have not performed well. In fact, the score cards of Senators and Congress members are so dismal; those scoundrels would be given the pink slip if they'd had real jobs.

Why can't these folks vote on one bill at a time on the House and Senate floor? Politicians routinely add pork to Senate and House Bills, so they become as effective as giving free corn on the cob to a toothless man.

# CHAPTER EIGHT

## ABSENTEE BALLOTS?

Elected officials all promise to be our collective voice in return for our vote. They need to be present to vote on the issues. You can't keep a job if you're chronically absent or late. The same should apply to legislators. They need to have their butts in the chair and vote how their constituents want them to vote.

## MIGHTY MEDIA

The media is far too influential. It should allow us to know about events, not interpret them for us. One could argue that the media-biased questions kick started the backbiting, fighting, and other elementary school aged displays of despicable taste and rhetoric which are an embarrassment.

A former Secretary of State sent gobs of emails on a private server even after the State Department said that wasn't kosher.

The D.C. players seem to win by cheating. Many elected officials tout, "if you're fed up with D.C., vote for me". All talk. No action. Nothing much ever changes. Sound familiar?

The guy whom many people feel comes with some fresh ideas having not been involved as a Washington insider is making headlines. He does not pull any punches in the Board Room. However, such antics don't play as well in the Political Mainstream, where prepared statements and memorized lines are the norm.

He reminds me of the character "The Beast" from the Disney children's classic movie "Beauty and the Beast." Deep down inside, The Beast is kind and has a good heart, but for many reasons we may not understand, he often comes across as a bull in a china shop. A leader can be tough on any stance without berating, belittling or disrespecting the opposition.

## LESSON FROM THE PAST

During the surrender of Japan at the end of WWII, American leadership was firm, yet respectful of the leadership of Japan. The process was handled with dignity, grace, and respect even though atrocities had been committed by the Japanese.

Similarly, many passionate supporters feel a business savvy candidate has sound ideas on how to make America Great Again.

When you own the company, you can be direct, to the point and forego political correctness. Heck, you can even be narcissistic and terse.

But those tactics are about as effective as screaming at a deaf person behind their back in a presidential campaign.

"The Donald" using his familiar boss tack, unintentionally provides continuous fodder for Democrats to take him to task by using his matter-of-fact vernacular to put a political spin on the issues and creating inflammatory claims.

Trump falls right in and retaliates like he's Mohammed Ali. Democrats and opposing Republicans are putting the spin on his words and using them to create fear and hurt feelings with many groups of people. His opponents paint a picture of him as a hater, a racist, a bigot, and fascist. Worse, they may even accuse him of wearing spray-on hair!

## M-O-N-E-Y

Money talks. Hillary is outspending the boys. Can these schoolboy ruffians overcome a woman's big purse?

## DON'T LET ISSUES INTERFERE WITH A GOOD JAB

Rocky Balboa is back in the recent movie "Creed", but TV viewers are also feeling like they're ringside when watching political debates.

Issues have actually taken a back seat as the main events are candidates duking it out, school yard bully style, especially on the Republican side. The grade school behavior not only takes away from the dignity of the elections but alienates new or open-minded voters.

Dale Carnegie would suggest that if you want to win friends and influence people, calling those you disagree with names and putting them down, isn't the best approach.

Too many people use the "gotcha" mentality, which is dangerous. It carries treacherous consequences for our country. It only creates a hostile environment at town hall meetings.

Pomp and circumstance belongs where it was intended, at graduation ceremonies.

Then there's the "cool kids" vs. the nerds. Since the onset of TV, candidates are often judged by looks and/or if they looked comfortable enough to be presidential. People make decisions based on physical attributes. Bah!

Unfortunately, a candidate's pride can cause them to make ridiculous statements played out ad nauseam by the media.

Americans want better answers, more accurate answers, and more concise answers; all with much less rhetoric and more respect, dignity, and acceptance for all. But accountability needs to be embraced by all parties.

## ARE THEY MAKING THIS UP?

Candidates are almost hand feeding spin opportunities to opponents. There is something fundamentally wrong when a candidate is having a levity moment with an enthusiastic rally crowd and says "... raise your hand and promise you will vote for me", and opponents equate this to invoking the same allegiance Nazi Party supporters gave Hitler during his rise to power. That is just wrong, dude!

If a person shouts down a candidate and refuses to leave, that is naughty behavior. In America every person has the right to free speech. To impede this is a big no-no. If you oppose a particular person's views you can hold signs in protest but keep a respectful distance.

Bring your signs but be nice. As any kindergarten teacher knows, don't pop off to others with different ideas.

Protestors refusing to leave when asked, instead cry "Wolf!" "Nazi!" "He's assaulting me, mommy!" Waah!

# CHAPTER NINE

## BLAME THE RESEARCHER...

*We interrupt this book to bring you a special news bulletin: The following material is for mature audiences only. By that, I mean those who passed basic algebra, philosophy, or prehistoric political science; or any other advanced course. For the rest of you, don't worry, you don't have to "evoke" John Nash...*

## VOTING PARADOX

Condorcet's paradox (the voting paradox) is a situation noted by the Marquis de Condorcet in the late 18th century.

Suppose we have three candidates, A, B, and C. There are three voters with preferences as follows (candidates being listed left-to-right for each voter in decreasing order of preference):

| Voter | 1st preference | 2nd preference | 3rd preference |
|-------|---------------|----------------|----------------|
| Voter 1 | A | B | C |
| Voter 2 | B | C | A |
| Voter 3 | C | A | B |

If C is chosen as the winner, it can be argued that B should win instead, since two voters (1 and 2) prefer B to C and only one voter (3) prefers C to B. However, by the same argument A is preferred to B, and C is preferred to A, by a margin of two to one on each occasion. Thus the society's preferences show cycling: A is preferred over B which is preferred over C which is preferred over A. A paradoxical feature of relations between the voters' preferences described above is that although the majority of voters agree that A is preferable to B, B to C, and C to A, all three coefficients of rank correlations between the voters' preferences are negative (namely, -.5), as calculated with Spearman's rank correlation coefficient formula designed by Charles Spearman much later.

Don't get discouraged with all this heavy duty reading. Read on. As you can see, figuring out the political process is complicated, frustrating, and...

## PARADOXAL CONDITION

Suppose that x is the fraction of voters who prefer A over B and that Y is the fraction of voters who prefer B over C. It has been shown that the fraction z of voters who prefer A over C is always at least $(x + y - 1)$. Since the paradox (a majority preferring Cover A) requires $z < 1/2$, a necessary condition for the paradox is best explained by the following equation:

$$x+y-1 \leq z < 1/2 \quad \text{and hence} \quad x+y < 3/2.$$

Take a deep breath if you didn't get all that... just take two aspirin and call our researcher in the morning!

## NO ONE CAN WIN?

When a Condorcet method is used to determine an election with three or more candidates, there is no fair resolution. Someone who is a front runner in the first round can get knocked out by those who jump ship and vote for the other candidate(s) the next time.

The structure of the two stages makes a difference for whether A, B or C is the ultimate winner.

Likewise, the structure of a sequence of votes in a legislature can be manipulated by the person arranging the votes, to ensure his preferred outcome.

In summary, voters should make a tactical or strategic vote based on what is important to them. Unfortunately people from both major parties are often swayed to vote for a particular candidate based on party preference.

Some will assert that TV talking heads will try to influence voters. As of this writing, it is not clear if Republicans will only support an insider.

If Republicans end up in an Open Convention... Condorcet and John Nash may have to rise from the grave and explain the situation. Either, way, Epic Fail for the Elephant Party.

## POLITICAL POWDER KEG?

Our research team concluded that the Republican Party is close to imploding and the Democratic Party is on thin ice.

## CHAPTER TEN

# $6 BILLION.

# Yep.

### SAY IT OUT LOUD, AND POP THE "B" IN BILLION FOR EMPHASIS!

*That's the total amount spent on the last presidential election; back in the olden days of 2012... So, that would be like, way more money nowadays, right?*

*According to an estimate by the non-partisan Center for Responsive Politics, that big, fat $6 BILLION is still $700 million more than the previous "most expensive election" in history—2008—and includes money spent by the campaigns, outside groups, and independent organizations.*

***$970 million*** *The estimated amount spent by outside groups during the 2012 cycle, according to Federal Election Commission data.*

## WHERE THE $$$ COMES FROM...

Joe Cocker would agree, we all need a little help from our friends... so, here's the rundown on campaign funding (inside from the party, or outside from Political Action Committees and special interest groups, AS OF MID MARCH 2016.)

### HILLARY CLINTON (D)

$ 57,748,407.....OUTSIDE
$154,146,063.....INSIDE

### TED CRUZ (R)

$50,743,053.....OUTSIDE
$66,199,643.....INSIDE

### BERNIE SANDERS (D)

$46,080........OUTSIDE
$96,311,423 INSIDE

### DONALD TRUMP (R)

$1,968,261.....OUTSIDE
$25,526,319 INSIDE

# CHAPTER ELEVEN

## AGE  G A P

It seems the age gap is divided. Looks like that gap is younger voters' support Bernie Sanders (known simply as "Bernie") and older Democrats support Hillary Clinton (known simply as "Hillary".)

On the other hand, Republican youths strongly favor Trump and many older ones are in the Cruz camp.

Does that mean Bernie is wooing youngsters with his promises of free health care, etc? Perhaps Trump is wooing young voters with his strong stands on immigration and his cutting sound bites that make his opponents appear weak and indecisive.

Cruz, with his Constitutionality, appeals to conservative older voters who like the idea of law and order. Hillary is a favorite among women and traditional liberal thinkers.

But the purpose of this book isn't to fall prey to vague stereotypes. In fact, breaking down male/female and social status and age/race distinctions isn't the purpose of this book.

We're here to get you the quick facts on how each candidate stands on the issues brought up in the 2016 election. A quick "YES" or "NO" from each candidate on the issues, so you don't have to plow through multiple biased sources plugging their man (or woman!)

But before we entirely leave the topic of age as it relates to voters, let me point out:

John's oldest son turned 18 during the writing of this book. He eagerly anticipated registering to vote, a rite of passage reserved for those 18 and older. Many of his fellow high school senior classmates are also coming of age and intending to vote. He was surprised at how many of them are singing the praises of Bernie Sanders.

John's son asked several classmates why they support "Bernie" as he's known on his signs and campaign material.

"He's a cute old man," one girl gushed.

"Why are you against Trump?" my son countered (he's a Trump man).

"Because he's gonna make all the Muslims leave our country, and that's just mean."

Well, now you have it, folks.

But before you think I'm just being a crabby old man, I entered a political conversation with a 20 something co-worker recently. The young man was quite interested in politics; he asked what my views were and continued a lively and interested conversation. "I wish I could find out everyone's political views before I get to know their name," he said. "I'm still making up my mind about how I think about things."

He seemed genuinely interested in my answers to his questions about health care, immigration, the economy and other issues. We both happened to be working setting up a banquet for a political rally, and the young co-worker of mine introduced himself to one of the candidates and eagerly read the candidates' bio.

We need more interested young people like that. I believe many young people are interested in politics, and several look beyond the superficial. I may or may not agree with their deductions, but if they are trying to stay informed, more power to them.

# WHY CANDIDATES CAN'T WIN

Candidate X wins a national election and is eager to represent constituents back home.

Then someone knocks on his new office door in Washington, D.C. The Good Candidate, now Officeholder, sits on the edge of his seat while the Party Leader parks stiffly across from him.

"Welcome to the club. Now that you've won, the party expects you to pay your dues. Here's a list of rich folks in your voting district. Hit them up for cash. Lots of it. $2 million bucks during the next quarter. If you don't ... well... we can't support you again."

"But, how am I supposed to do all the wonderful things I promised to do to get elected if I'm spending all my time calling and begging for money?"

The Party Leader shrugs. "Hire a team of monkeys to call your rich voters during dinner, interrupt their meetings, double up on calls to cell phones, home numbers, office numbers, personal e-mails, anything you can do to pay for your next campaign. You do wanna get re-elected and keep your cushy benefits, don't you?"

Our Good Candidate X is in a quandary... Is running for re-election worth it under these sell out conditions? Is chasing the money from the big companies and rich voters really the only priority? What about doing the will of the people, as promised in the original campaign?

Next thing you know, we have another D.C. convert to the campaign finance system, the hostile regime currently keeping lawmakers from being effective and turning them into liars.

The story above is happening every day, folks. It's exactly why government is failing.

## BUT WAIT, THERE'S HOPE!

In fact, it's already taking place. Another way of funding campaigns. Examples are the State of Maine, and the cities of New York and Seattle. In those places, citizen funded election programs match funds and offer vouchers to voters, allowing them to support the candidate of their choice without forcing the candidate to waste precious time raising money instead of doing their job to serve the public.

We, your handsome and dedicated co-authors, Greg and John, urge you, the voter/reader, to Google "Dialing for Dollars" and get a whiff of what we're talking about! You're on the trail, sic 'em!

"An educated voter will keep elected officials in check, creating common sense voter consistency in the elected official succession process by upholding Constitutional rights. Failure to honor this privilege by not studying the issues creates 'ignorant' voters who jeopardize the many freedoms we have enjoyed. If a free people apathetically decide not to vote or vote for myopic reasons, we will eventually erode the free election process." —Greg Daniels

## PAC VS. BIG BOYS

Remember that kid in school who wouldn't back down to the school bully, even though they could beat the tar out of him?

That's how one lil' ol' Political Action Committee (PAC) known as Citizens United (CU) is standing up to the Big Boys, the large corporations. They're talking smack against the way large companies support candidates. They say it's a violation of free speech to let a big company influence lawmakers with dollars.

The schoolyard brawl began in 2008. CU wanted to use TV ads against a certain candidate, but were told this would violate an act banning ads that mention candidates by name too soon before an election.

In 2009, CU sued the Federal Election Commission to eliminate restrictions on how corporations can spend money in elections.

In a 5-4 ruling, the Justices declared government restriction on independent political spending by corporations and unions unconstitutional. The decision overturned a century old law which allowed the government to regulate spending on campaign influencers such as media.

Five Supremes argued and WON:

- barring independent political spending amounts to squelching free speech protected by the First Amendment.
- the First Amendment protects not just a person's right to speak, but the act of speech itself, regardless of the speaker. Therefore the First Amendment protects the

speech of corporations and unions, whether we consider them people or not.

- although government has the authority to prevent corruption or "the appearance of corruption," it has no place in determining whether large political expenditures are either of those things, so it may not impose spending limits on that basis.
- the public has the right to hear all available information, and spending limits prevent information from reaching the public.

Four Supremes argued and LOST:

the First Amendment protects only individual speech.

- government may prevent corruption, and campaign spending can be corrupt when it buys influence over legislators. Therefore government may impose spending limits on corporations and unions.
- government may prevent the appearance of corruption, which undermines public confidence in democracy. Limits on corporate and union political spending are an expression of that authority.
- the public has the right to hear all available information, and when corporations spend money individuals can't match, messages from corporations drown out messages from others, and that information fails to reach the public.

Even prior to the 2008 elections, PAC spending nearly tripled from 2004 to 2008. The same exponential increase was realized between 2008 and 2012. The trend of big money influencers continues at an exponential pace as the 2016 campaign continues. PAC influence has taken on a life of its own.

Opponents of this legislation have been busy in the seven years since passage of this ruling.  Ten states have already passed measures in opposition to CU. More states are crafting legislation.  Since this book is about "the election process", we can only recommend readers check out the many organizations trying to sponsor legislation to overturn this ruling.

To remain unbiased, we recommend you do your own research.  For this subject, go to your favorite browser and enter "Citizens United". This will be time consuming, so bring your snacks and favorite beverage. Get as comfy as possible, but don't lull yourself to sleep. Too many voters are already guilty of that! You want to be a superior reader/voter of the Greg-John path to "informaty," that is our made up word for

becoming a better informed voter than your neighbor (you'll have bragging rights!)

Better still, you'll be part of the change everyone keeps talking about but never accomplishes. It's time to change the way we learn; don't let yourself get suckered into the lie that no one can make a difference. You can. You already are by reading this. Good voter! Two Scooby snacks for you!

When you learn, you grow. Share your newfound findings with us at OverTheTopPublications@gmail.com. Thanks for being a good citizen!

# MORE RESOURCES

**Issues from an Evangelical Christian Perspective:**
www.afa.net
www.citizenlink.org
www.faithandfamily.com

www.frc.org
iVoteValues.org

**Candidate Positions on Election Issues:**
www.votesmart.org
www.ontheissues.org

**Election News:**
www.bpnews.net
www.cnn.com
www.cnsnews.com
www.foxnews.com
www.onenewsnow.com
www.realclearpolitics.com
www.usatoday.com

# THE WRAP UP

## What does all this mean?

Never in U.S. history has the presidential race been so mangled with legal landmines. As of this writing, Republican candidates seem incapable of gathering enough electoral votes for the RNC nomination. Democrats, similarly, are in a tangle with a "lead" candidate trailing in popularity to an underdog. The outcome is murky at best. We can't sit back. We must act. Now!

## Where do we go from here?

- All voters, Democrat and Republican, must unite as one to stand up for a new presidential selection process if we are to avoid the stalemate we live in
- Contact your Congress member and share the ideas in this book and other ideas you have with them

## Why is it important?

- If we don't act now, our constitution could be jeopardized by players seeking self-interest over protocol, washing out any possibility of future stability in selecting our president
- Disgruntled voters on both sides may split off into further isolation, apathy, or third party options that continue the stalemate process and hinder the nation

# THE CURE

## Know your candidates

- Research their websites and ask them for their voting records on issues you find important
- Demand answers to questions you have. Meet office holders and office seekers every chance you get.
- If you feel inclined, run for office or assist in a campaign

## Know your criterion

- What are you looking for in a candidate? Go beyond personality and looks. Come on, be an educated voter! Why do you want a certain candidate? Is it just to knock out the one you DON'T want? Never vote blind. Learn, research, be responsible. Teach your kids and grandkids to do the same. Show them how the political game works and play to win!

Thanks for reading. Regardless of the 2016 election outcome, the American voters are officially on notice—there are indeed, in our humble, yet qualified opinion, better ways to conduct a presidential campaign. See you in 2020!

Roll Ending Credits...

Happy Voting,
Greg and John